D1189866

EXPLORING
THEATER

Directing in Theater

Jeri Freedman

Cavendish
Square

New York

Published in 2017 by Cavendish Square Publishing, LLC
243 5th Avenue, Suite 136, New York, NY 10016

Library of Congress Cataloging-in-Publication Data

Names: Freedman, Jeri.
Title: Directing in theater / Jeri Freedman.
Description: New York : Cavendish Square Publishing, 2017. | Series: Exploring theater | Includes index.
Identifiers: ISBN 9781502622839 (library bound) | ISBN 9781502622846 (ebook)
Subjects: LCSH: Theater--Production and direction--Juvenile literature. | Theater--Juvenile literature.
Classification: LCC PN2053.F74 2017 | DDC 792.02'32--dc23

Editorial Director: David McNamara
Editor: Fletcher Doyle
Copy Editor: Nathan Heidelberger
Associate Art Director: Amy Greenan
Designer: Joseph Macri
Production Coordinator: Karol Szymczuk
Photo Research: J8 Media

Printed in the United States of America

CONTENTS

One of the responsibilities of a director is to provide instructions to actors during the rehearsal of a play.

CHAPTER ONE

THE SKILLS OF THE DIRECTOR

It is the director's job to bring together all the elements that go into making a play a reality on the stage. The director chooses and rehearses actors, **blocks** the play (sets the actors' movements), and works with the technical crew, including the **set** designer, lighting and sound technicians, costumers and makeup artists, and the conductor if the play is a musical. In high school and some community theaters, the director may also oversee the publicity to advertise the play.

In a high school setting, the role of director is often filled by a teacher or volunteer. A student is often chosen to be an assistant director or stage manager. This person assists the director during **preproduction** activities and oversees backstage activities during performances. Stage managing is an excellent opportunity to learn the skills of a director. If the school has a drama club in which students put on their own plays, or put on a play as a fundraising activity for a school or charity event, a student might direct in his or her own right. In some schools, seniors are given the opportunity to put on plays, including directing them.

Some community theaters maintain permanent facilities, and they are always in need of talented people to run them.

Community theaters are local theaters found in cities and towns around the country. There are many types of community theaters. Some community theater consists of performances put on by local amateur performers in rented or donated venues such as school auditoriums, or town or local organization halls. This type of community theater often starts with an individual who wishes to direct plays. This person picks the play, **auditions** and rehearses the actors, and oversees the technical phases of the production. The director in this case may put on plays on a regular basis all year round or seasonally. A second type of community theater consists of a permanent company of actors. This type of group is often called something like The [*Name of Town*] Players. A community theater may have a permanent facility or rent a local hall or auditorium. In this type of community theater, the director, actors, and crew will have day jobs (unless they are retired) and put on plays in their spare time. A community theater can also have a large permanent facility and a full-time staff, and it may employ professional actors or a combination of professional and local actors for performances in the community. Many "summer theaters" fall into this category. The professional community theater may be headed by a director or by a producer who hires a director for each play the theater produces. Directors in community theaters may work with all local amateur actors, a combination of amateur and professional actors, or professional actors and student actors. Most community theaters are nonprofit organizations. Many offer training classes for students in addition to putting on plays.

The Director's Skills

A theatrical director needs a variety of skills to succeed—and not go crazy—during the process of putting on a play. These include analytical, technical, creative, and interpersonal skills.

Analytical Skills

Analytical skills are critical for a director. These skills come into play in several ways. Unless the director is hired by a community theater to put on a particular play, the first thing a director has to do is choose a play. This process requires a director to analyze the pool of available actors and the audience for whom the play will be performed. Next, the director must consider potential plays to decide which would be appropriate for the theater's resources and audience. After the play is selected, the director must analyze the play to find the elements that will have an emotional impact on the audience. It is these elements that will make the performance successful. The director must examine the characters in the play and then consider the performance skills and personal characteristics of the actors in the company, or those who audition, in order to find those best suited to the roles. The director must also evaluate the technical elements that will be required, such as the sets, costumes, lighting, and sound effects that will best enhance the presentation of the play.

Technical Skills

The director needs a variety of technical skills in order to stage the play, including blocking (placement of actors), rehearsal techniques, and creating schedules and cue sheets, among others. Directors need to understand how emotion, gesture, movement, and vocal expression are used by actors to create an effective performance. These skills can be learned from drama courses, books on directing, working as a stage manager or assistant director in school or community theater productions, or being a student intern at a professional community theater. In addition, it is valuable for the director to understand public relations and marketing techniques for advertising and promoting the performance so that the public knows about it and wants to attend.

Interpersonal Skills

Interpersonal skills are those that allow a person to work well with others to accomplish tasks and achieve a goal. Some of the characteristics required to be a successful director are patience, fortitude, self-discipline, organizational ability, and problem-solving skills. Patience is often required when actors don't learn their lines quickly enough, or when problems arise with sets, costumes, or other technical elements.

The director must often work hard with an actor to overcome problems with his or her performance. It may take imagination to come up with creative ways to convey the director's vision for the role, or the play as a whole, to the actor. Patience must be tempered, however, with the ability and authority to get people to do what is necessary. Not understanding the nuances of a role is one thing—not bothering to learn one's lines or show up on time for rehearsal is another.

Self-discipline means that the director does what is necessary to pull the play together, even when no one is requiring him or her to do so. The director has to be prepared to work long hours when no one is forcing him or her to do so. This may mean not engaging in other activities that he or she would prefer to be doing until the work on the play is over. Organizational skills allow the director to manage his or her time and schedule. Having organizational skills means being able to establish when various elements such as costumes, lighting, props, scenery, and the like, need to be completed, and then to assign and monitor tasks necessary to ensure that everything is ready on time. Time-management skills allow a director to accomplish all this and still have time to meet the demands of other aspects of his or her life. This means being able to keep track of everything that needs to be done and the time that it must be done by. The director must be able to prioritize tasks and delegate work when necessary.

Fortitude means that the director has the ability to persevere, even when all types of problems arise while preparing to put on a play—and they always do. The director must be able to overcome obstacles, solve problems, and make choices without becoming overwhelmed. The ability to deal with stress is important for anyone leading a project. Problem-solving skills allow the director to analyze a situation and identify possible solutions or alternatives. Sometimes a problem cannot be solved by the director alone. Teachers or other professionals whom one can ask for advice are valuable resources. A director needs to know when to ask for assistance and the appropriate people to ask for assistance.

Creativity

In the final analysis, directing is about using actors, lighting, setting, costumes, music, and other elements to create a play that has an emotional impact on an audience. The result may be funny, sad, touching, or delightful, but it must affect the audience to be successful. To accomplish this, directors must have

Directors must be able to come up with creative solutions for performances that take place in nontraditional settings, such as outdoor settings.

creative vision and use their skills to creative effect. Where the director places actors in relation to each other; the tone he or she has them take when speaking; and the type of lighting, costumes, and sets the director uses all contribute to attaining a specific effect. Before the director even begins casting a play, he or she must go through the script page by page and develop an overall picture of the effect on the audience he or she wants the play to achieve. The director then needs to think about all the elements that will go into achieving that effect. For example, if you were directing Shakespeare's *Macbeth*, would you use dark costumes and sets—to emphasize the mysterious and dramatic aspects of the play and the horror of the murder—or would you use historically accurate costumes and sets and present the play as a historical drama? Or would you set the play in a modern time period and aim for relevance to a contemporary political situation?

The creative decisions of the director determine the audience's perception of a play. To understand all the elements that a director must work with, you might want to attend some community and summer theater plays and observe how the director uses lighting, costumes, sets, and sound to create particular effects on the audience. Some theaters have special pricing for students or free access in return for volunteering as an **usher**.

Developing Directing Skills

High school provides an opportunity to develop two types of skills that can help one be a successful director. The first type of skill involves general knowledge. Directing plays requires a knowledge of both literature and language. English courses provide an opportunity to learn the rules of grammar and syntax, which allow students to understand how language works. Language skills also enable one to speak and write clearly and correctly, which minimizes misunderstanding when directing actors. They also help a director appear professional when speaking to members of the community from whom he or she may be seeking financial support, venues in which to perform, or materials for the production. Classes in history are useful for understanding the context in which plays that are not contemporary take place and for a sense of setting, costumes, and props. A basic knowledge of math will help when preparing and tracking a budget.

A second type of education that may be available is courses that teach skills directly related to the performing arts. If your school has a drama club or a course in drama, take the opportunity to learn specific aspects of theater and their terminology. Even if your school only teaches acting, not directing, the experience can help you understand the elements that go into creating a moving performance, which in turn will allow you to get the best performance from actors. If you cannot take drama courses at your school, you may be able to take such courses at one of the community or summer theaters in your area. Many theaters supplement their income by offering classes in acting and other aspects of theatrical production.

Even if you don't want to perform in front of an audience, high school productions and other events can provide useful experience. If a teacher is directing a school play, see if there is a need for a stage manager to assist with the production. If not, volunteer for other behind-the-scenes work. This will let you observe firsthand the elements that go into directing a play. While you are in high school, you can also take advantage of internship opportunities to gain experience. Contact the local theaters in your area, including community and summer theaters, and ask if they have student intern positions. These are unpaid positions in which students perform a variety of behind-the-scenes tasks. Larger community and summer theaters often employ professional actors and staff; they can provide invaluable information.

Construction crewmembers prepare the flats that will provide the setting for the play being produced.

The director instructs the student crew on the mood or style wanted for the background for a scene.

CHAPTER TWO

HEAD OF A TEAM

The director is the leader of the team that puts on the play. As a leader, the director must be able to keep a group working constructively toward its goal, even when a project encounters an obstacle or the director makes an unpopular decision. Sooner or later the director will have to deal with conflict within the group and still be able to keep the project on track. The first step in producing the play is to forge a team from the individuals involved.

The Players and the Crew

The director works with two groups of people. One group is the cast, which consists of the actors actually performing the play. The other is the crew, which includes all those who fulfill technical functions. The crew might include some or all of the following, depending on the size of the production:

- Stage manager: The person who oversees the activities that go on backstage during a performance.

- Lighting technician: The person who sets

up the lights that will be used during the performance. If lighting changes during the play, he or she may also control the lights during the performance.

- Sound technician: This person designs and performs sound effects.

- Costumer: This person assembles or makes the clothing that the actors wear.

- Set designer/construction crew: These people build and paint the set. They may also collect furniture for the set.

- Props master: This person assembles the props required and makes sure they are set up for use during rehearsals and the performance.

- Makeup artist: In many community theaters, actors do their own makeup. However, some types of performances, such as holiday or historical plays, might require a person who knows how to do special-effects makeup.

- Stagehands: These people change the set, if necessary, for different scenes during the performance.

A high school or community theater may not use these formal names for the crewmembers, but it will still require people to fill these roles in order to put on the play.

The director must make sure that the members of the cast work well together to put on a seamless performance. He or she must work with the crew to

The lighting crew hangs and focuses lights according to the lighting designer's plan.

ensure that all the technical elements come together in the right way during the performance. In addition, the director must see to it that the cast and crew respect each other and work together **harmoniously**.

Motivating the Cast and Crew

When directing community or high school theater productions, the director most likely will be working with amateur actors and a volunteer crew. In most cases, no one involved with the production is being paid. Therefore, the director must find other means of persuading actors and crew to show up when required and perform the tasks they need to do. Many of these people also face the demands of a day job and/or family commitments. One way to **motivate** them is to create a sense that all the participants in the production belong to a team. People usually desire to support people they view as friends and do not want to let them down. The director must also create a sense of the play's importance to the group so that members give it priority among their responsibilities. The director needs to get the participants excited about the project.

Providing recognition and praise encourages people to want to participate and do their best. On television, directors are often portrayed as autocratic tyrants who force their will on the cast and crew. This is not the way most directors work in real life—and it certainly won't work with people who are not receiving large amounts of money to put up with a director who takes this approach. Directors do have to give instructions to the cast and crew and to correct their mistakes, but successful directors know how to do this in a productive way that creates an atmosphere of cooperation, not discord.

Actors act because they crave attention and praise. It is important for the director to put aside his or her own desire for recognition and instead praise the cast (and crew) when they do a good job. The director can encourage actors to support and help each other, rather than compete for attention, by praising those who help other actors. This approach will make the lead actors and those with experience more likely to assist those who are less experienced.

At the end of each rehearsal, the director should thank the actors for their hard work. He or she should also thank the crew when they complete a project. Showing appreciation makes people feel valued and reduces competition among them for recognition. Providing a social element to group work helps people relax and become friendly with each other. For example, one might order pizza for the cast during the first read-through together of the script, or for the crew when they are working all day on the weekend.

Nurturing Creativity

Actors may come from diverse backgrounds. In community theater, members of a cast might include experienced retired actors, acting students, local actors who perform as extras in TV shows or movies that are made on location in their city, and employees in a variety of fields who act as a hobby. In a high school production, students might come from a variety of ethnic and cultural backgrounds. A director must ensure that people who have different levels of experience, different types of personalities, and different backgrounds feel comfortable together.

The director must create an environment in which everyone feels free to express their ideas. This means

A director must ensure that actors work together even when they have different approaches to a scene.

keeping more experienced actors from dominating those less experienced, and ensuring that the less experienced actors feel confident when making suggestions about their role and characters. The director must make sure that actors can express their ideas without being criticized by others in the group.

Conflict

Many types of conflict can occur within groups, including theater organizations, and the director must be able to deal with them. Sometimes it is necessary to correct people when directing. The director must learn to do this in a way that is nonthreatening and constructive rather than merely critical. When problems occur or issues arise with the cast or crew, the director must be able to discuss these with the person or persons involved without blaming them. If people are not blamed, they are more likely to cooperate in fixing the problem. It's more productive to address a problem or mistake as something that needs to be fixed by working together. Creating a positive environment makes actors and crewmembers more enthusiastic about participating in the project and more likely to show up and do their jobs reliably.

The director may be confronted with issues such as actors attempting to dominate the group, people whose attitude is chronically negative, and arguments. Sometimes one of the cast members will be a pessimist who constantly explains why a suggested approach is wrong or won't work. This type of attitude can upset other cast members and may disrupt the entire project if others are convinced by this negative point of view. Often the director in a community theater does not have a wide choice of people to play a given role because of the character's age or physical characteristics and the limited number of people who wish to participate. Therefore, replacing a problematic person may not be possible. In this case, the director must neutralize

A director sometimes must diffuse a confrontation between student actors.

the person's negative attitude. One approach is to counteract the negative viewpoint by acknowledging that it may or may not be true, then requesting ideas on how the approach might work. Let the positive actors try it their way. This will provide an opportunity to demonstrate that the approach can work, and rewarding positive behavior makes the point that being positive gets one more attention than being negative.

Confrontations can occur if one person starts harassing another, or two people start arguing. This is more likely to happen in a high school rehearsal among young people who haven't learned to control their emotions. Sometimes conflicts occur between actors and crewmembers who are trying to get their job done. Sometimes two people are competing for attention. Sometimes they have issues that have nothing to do with the play; these can affect their personal relationship and their ability to work together.

It's best to stop confrontations immediately, before they get out of control. If two people start exchanging nasty comments, the director can intercede, attempting to direct their attention back to the project. If there appears to be a real problem that will derail the production, the director can take the people involved aside or to a different room. In privacy, the leader can then discuss the problem with them, listening to both sides of the story. The director can work with them to arrive at a mutually agreeable solution, make a decision on how the issue in question should be approached for the good of the play, or, if the problem is personal, he or she can get them to agree to leave their baggage outside the rehearsal room and concentrate on the play when they're there.

People often cause problems because they feel insecure. They want attention and need to feel important. Therefore, one of the most successful approaches to people who cause problems is to coopt them. In this approach, the director redirects them from being disruptive to being constructive by putting them in charge of some area of the production. Acknowledging the work they are doing and making them feel important can often turn them into contributors who have a vested interest in the success of their project.

Balancing Avocation and Work/School

The director of a high school or community theater play is very busy. Rehearsals happen on several evenings or weekends, and the director needs to work out the details of costumes, lighting, the set, and other aspects of the play with the crew, and oversee the construction and setup. Although not all actors are needed at every rehearsal, the director certainly is. It's easy to turn an **avocation**—directing a play—into a nearly full-time job. When directing a play, it's important to balance the demands of the project with the demands of employment or schoolwork. One can't lose focus on the fact that the daytime activities are important for one's present and future welfare. One of the key aspects of putting on a play as an avocation is keeping the project manageable. It's necessary to make sure that the vision for the finished project is achievable in the time available. One needs to be realistic about how long it's going to take to get the play ready, and schedule it far enough in advance to allow time for the required number of rehearsals and the creation of all the sets, costumes, and props.

Going to school and directing a play require managing one's time carefully. Make a weekly schedule so you know in advance when you have to accomplish projects both at home and at the theater. Plan what you will do if you suddenly get a large school or work project and need more time for non-directing activities. Appoint a person as assistant director or stage manager and arrange for him or her to split some responsibilities with you if necessary. Make a daily to-do list beginning with the most critical activities, then delegate the less important tasks.

Eat well, exercise, and get adequate sleep. This will keep you healthy and in good shape to deal effectively with the demands of school/work and your avocation. Enjoy what you're doing. Creating a theatrical production should be enjoyable for you and the other people working on it.

The director's vision for the play defines
every aspect of a play from the costumes
and sets to the actors' performances.

CHAPTER THREE

DIRECTING THE PLAY

T here are three stages to the play production process: preproduction, rehearsal, and show time. The director has different tasks during each of these phases.

Preproduction

The first thing the director must do is become familiar with the play. He or she begins by reading the script and making notes. Typically the director will read the script multiple times and make notes on his or her vision of the characters and their relationships. The director must have a clear idea of the characters before he or she can begin to cast the play. The director may also make some notes about the physical aspects of the play, such as sets, props, costumes, and lighting.

Before directors can do their job, they must have a clear idea of how they want to present the play, what its key focus is, and who the characters are. Plays captivate audiences not just because of what the actors say and do, but because of why they do it. The director has to study the characters in the play and decide what their motivations are. If a character commits a crime, joins the army, or marries someone, why does he or she do it? Is the girl who gets married head over heels in love, looking for security, or trying to get away from an abusive home life? Sometimes the answer to such questions is spelled out in the script. At other times, it's not clear from what's written on the page. In this case, the director must consider the overall message of the play—what theme is the playwright trying to convey? The choices the director makes in terms of motivation for the characters will influence his or her choice of actors to fill the roles.

Before a director can begin directing the play, he or she must take stock of the resources that are available. The director must evaluate the space in which the play is to be staged. How large are the stage and the backstage area? The size of these areas will affect the size and style of the set and how scene and costume changes are to be handled. Similarly, the size of the auditorium or audience seating area will affect the acoustics—that is, how easy or difficult it is to hear the actors. It's also necessary to find out if the theater or auditorium is going to be used for other purposes during the period when the play is going to be rehearsed. If so, the dates when it is not available will need to be incorporated into the director's rehearsal schedule. What type of lights and sound equipment are available? Some theaters and school auditoriums have lights and sound equipment that the director can use. For other venues, equipment may have to be rented, and the director will need to find out what equipment is available from the rental sources in the area.

The director needs to draw up a budget. He or she needs to find out how much it costs to rent costumes or buy materials to make them, make props, and buy materials to build the set. Often, furniture is borrowed for school and community theater plays, but certain pieces may have to be purchased at yard sales or flea markets. The cost of lights and sound equipment is also included in the budget if these are not available on-site. A royalty may have to be paid for the right to use a play. Copying costs for flyers, programs, and tickets need to be considered as well. If the play is being held in a location that the group is renting, the rental fee must also be included. After the budget is complete, the director must track expenditures to make sure the cost doesn't exceed the money estimated to cover it.

Once the director has a vision for the play, it's time to assemble a cast and crew. The director assembles the cast by auditioning actors. First, the director must get the word out that a play is being cast. This can be accomplished by placing an online and/or print notice in newspapers and online job sites. It may be necessary to place notices for more than one week to attract a pool of actors large enough to choose from. Sending flyers to local university theater departments can be useful, as theater majors are often looking for opportunities to gain experience. Be sure to include the fact that you are also looking for volunteers to work on props, costumes, scenery, lighting, sound, and other areas. Post flyers in prominent places where people gather, such as the local library. A theater group may also have a list of people who regularly participate in performances. Those who would be

Community and school productions need to actively recruit actors of different ethnic and racial backgrounds to fill specific roles.

appropriate for a particular role can be contacted by email or phone.

Some community theaters have a volunteer producer who takes care of putting together the production team. However, the major decisions for the production elements still rest with the director, who is responsible for the overall vision for the play. Crewmembers may be paid staff or volunteers. If a theater does not have a group of volunteers who perform these roles, directors may have to recruit people they know to make costumes or help with other aspects of production. Each technical area needs one person to oversee that aspect of the production. Thus, the director needs a head costumer, set designer, lighting designer, and so on. Depending on the complexity of the requirements, some or all of these areas will require additional staff or volunteers to perform functions such as making scenery, props, or costumes.

Auditioning Actors

Most plays have roles for which the ethnicity of the character is not important. For example, a famous actress, a soldier, or a teacher could be of any background. Sometimes a play requires actors with specific characteristics. For instance, *Fences*, by August Wilson, is about a black couple dealing with racial prejudice in the 1950s. Therefore, the leads must be played by African Americans. The requirement for actors of a particular background should be specified on audition notices. For roles for which race or ethnicity is not relevant, notices should emphasize this fact, so that as many people as possible show up. A notice might say, "Required: 1 African American male aged 20–35, 1 African American female aged 20–35, 1 white female aged 30–45, 2 women any racial or ethnic background, 2 teenaged boys, any racial or ethnic background." This type of notice not only avoids the problem of having inappropriate people wasting their time showing up for auditions, but also encourages people to show up and audition, rather than assume that there are no roles for them.

School production auditions usually take place after school. Those for community theater usually take place in the evening or on a weekend day, so people who work can attend. During an audition, everyone trying out for a role is given the chance to read the part of that character from the script. In the case of the school and community theater, the director generally just asks the actors to read the dialogue of one or sometimes a couple of characters.

Before auditioning actors, the director chooses passages from the script for each character that is being cast. When actors show up for the audition, the director, or the director's assistant, gets their contact information, often by having them fill out a standard form. This form captures relevant information, including not only contact information but also physical characteristics such as age, height, and hair and eye color. It also asks for scheduling information—times when the person is available for rehearsals or is not available because of other activities. Many auditioning actors will bring a résumé listing other shows they have performed in and other relevant experience. Even if the director

The director should try to find a way for students not picked for onstage roles to participate.

doesn't cast them in this play, keeping this information in a file provides a pool of talent the director can contact to audition for other plays in the future.

The director may have an idea in mind of the type of person who is appropriate for each character. However, for school or community theater, the actors available to choose from are those who show up. The director may be able to call on actors he or she knows personally, but it is generally preferable to choose actors who care enough to come to an audition. Sometimes, none of the actors who audition are appropriate for a particular role. This is especially true of male roles, as more women than men tend to come to auditions. Finding actors to fill these roles may require some **ingenuity** on the part of the director. If the actors who audition do not match the director's **preconceived** notion of what the character looks like, the director will have to change his or her preconception and instead consider how it is possible to use a person with the characteristics of those auditioning in the role. In other words, how would the role work with each person auditioning in it? Who would bring the best characteristics to the role?

The director begins the audition process by telling the actors about the play and the characters. He or she then asks the actors to read for a particular part or parts. In some cases—for example, if the role is half of a married couple in the play—the director will ask two actors to read together. During the audition, the director is trying to get a feel for whether the actor would do well in the role. The director is concerned with several things. Can the actor say lines in a way that expresses emotion and sounds natural? Does he or she understand the intent of the passage? How would he or she fit with the other potential cast members? The ability to deliver lines effectively is more important than the actor's physical appearance in most cases. During the audition, the director makes notes on the actors' audition forms. These notes include the roles the actors might be appropriate for, as well as key points about their performances.

After all the actors have been auditioned, the director considers his or her notes and their performances. If there is more than one actor who is a possibility for a role, the director will hold **callbacks**. The actors under consideration will be asked to come back for a final round of auditions. At the callbacks, actors who might be cast together are asked to read together. This gives the director a chance to observe their chemistry and how they play off each other.

After the callbacks, the director makes a decision as to which actor is most appropriate for each role. The director or assistant director contacts the actors who auditioned and tells the people who were chosen that they were selected and when the first rehearsal is.

Planning the Production

Unless the theater company is large enough to have a producer, the director, in addition to casting the play, must find people to work on the crew. These may be people who responded to the flyers, contacts of the director, community members, or students not acting in the play. Once the major crew positions have all been filled, the director holds a production meeting with all the crew. The director provides them with copies of the play and discusses the time period, setting, and style of the production—realistic or abstract, for instance. The director explains the atmosphere he or she is trying to achieve (romantic or spooky, for example). These factors affect the way the sets, lighting, and costumes will be designed.

After the crewmembers have had a chance to consider what the director is trying to achieve, and to think of ideas, the director holds another production meeting at which they can present their ideas for how to realize the concept for the play. Sometimes the director will like an idea. Sometimes he or she will think it is inappropriate or not possible due to cost or time constraints. However, it is very important that the director give all the crewmembers time to express their ideas, and just as important that the crewmembers feel their ideas are appreciated. Like the people in the cast, those in the crew crave recognition for their efforts. Therefore, the director must create an atmosphere in which all members feel their input is welcome. The director should see that everyone gets the chance to present ideas and be heard out before others raise objections. Later, the director will meet individually with each technical head and decide which ideas to adopt.

Production

During the production phase, the actors perfect their parts. The crew creates the set, costumes, props, and other elements required.

The director must know how to use all the technical elements of theater for dramatic effect: sets, lighting, sound, and costumes. Lighting can be used to create atmosphere. Using dim lighting or colored gels over the theatrical lights can create a brooding atmosphere. Lighting different areas of the stage differently—for instance, making one area darker or lighter—can focus attention on a character located

Creative lighting, such as a spotlight, can be used to emphasize specific aspects of a performance.

in a particular area. Scenery can be used to **reinforce** characteristics. For instance, an actor can be placed at the top of a stairway where he towers over the other characters, or a piece of furniture can be used as a barrier between two characters.

Both the style and color of costumes say volumes about a character. Attention to detail is important with costumes. A middle-class character down on his luck might have worn spots or a patch on his clothes. A woman who wears a high-collar dress creates a different impression from one who wears a low-cut dress. Bright colors can be used to convey an outgoing or assertive personality, dark colors can be used to make a character appear somber or conservative, and a lacy white dress on a young woman conveys innocence.

Some plays require sound effects, which may be the sound of footsteps or wind outside, or a radio news announcement (a commonly used device in mysteries). How the sound is recorded can make a difference in the tone of a scene. If the news announcement is breaking up, this can raise a question as to whether the electricity is going to go out, leaving the characters helpless in the dark.

Blocking a Play

Blocking is the placement of actors on the stage. Where people are located in relation to each other tells the audience a lot about their relationship. Do people sit or stand near each other? Do all the characters stand in a cluster, except for one person who is isolated? Does one character get up and turn his back on another, or move away from another person?

Blocking begins before rehearsal. The director goes through the play and decides how he or she will place the players, and where they move into new arrangements during each scene, as their interactions

The characters' clothing influences the audience's perception of their personality, economic status, and relationships.

change. Another aspect of blocking is **business**. These are the activities the characters perform in the environment in which the play takes place. A bartender preparing drinks or cleaning the bar, a servant cleaning up a meal, and a hotel guest writing a letter are examples of business. Like blocking, business can be used to show the character's state of mind. The way the character performs the activity can show us that he or she is nervous, happy, sad, distracted, or resentful about doing it.

Rehearsals

For the director, the core activity of the production period is rehearsals. Typically, the director will run rehearsals several evenings or weekends each week for four to six weeks. A director of a major community theater may have rehearsals five evenings each week, but the exact number will vary with the size of the theater group, the numbers of actors in the cast, and the complexity of the play. While the director attends all the rehearsals, not all the actors do. Rehearsals, especially the early ones, may concentrate on certain scenes in the play, and only the actors in those scenes need to attend.

The director begins the rehearsal process by drawing up a schedule that shows which actors are needed when. The director consults the forms filled out by the actors to determine when they are available, and the final schedule is distributed to the cast.

In high school theater, all of the actors are inexperienced, and part of the director's job is to teach the student actors the basics of performing a play. In community theater, the actors may be all inexperienced actors, all experienced amateur or retired professional actors, or a mix of experienced and inexperienced actors. The latter scenario is the most common.

With inexperienced actors, the director needs to explain what "homework" actors have to do. They must think about who their characters are and what their relationships are with the other characters. New actors may need specific instruction from the director to do so. The director may need to help the

A director works with student actors to help them understand their characters' relationship.

actor get a handle on his or her character by pointing out elements such as the language the character uses and who the character's friends or enemies are in the play. Getting the actor thinking about the character's life creates "subtext." Subtext is all the underlying features of the character that affect the way the actor portrays him or her. For example, how does he or she look at the other characters? Does the character look them in the eye or glance away, avoiding their eyes? It is these types of nuances that the director is trying to draw out of the actors in their performance in order to give the play depth and reality.

SELLARS MARKET

Peter Sellars started directing plays while a college student and has gone on to a long and successful career. Sellars is known for his bold and unusual productions. As an undergraduate at Harvard University, he staged a version of Wagner's *Ring* cycle operas using puppets. He also directed Chekhov's *The Three Sisters* at the Loeb Drama Center in Cambridge, Massachusetts, and **avant-garde** productions of Shakespeare's *Antony and Cleopatra* and *King Lear*, before graduating from Harvard in 1979.

Director Peter Sellars is known for his innovative productions.

In 1980, he directed a production of George Frideric Handel's opera *Orlando*, set in outer space, at the American Repertory Theater in Cambridge, Massachusetts, which brought him national attention. From 1983 to 1984, he was director of the Boston

Shakespeare Company. He was director and manager of the American National Theater in Washington, DC, from 1984 to 1986.

"Since I was a kid starting out, I've tried to do work based on subject matter that is meaningful to people," he told the *Guardian*.

He has also placed famous operas in contemporary settings because he thinks the themes of the music can't be bound by a time period. In the late 1980s, his productions of Mozart's operas *Così fan tutte*, set in a diner on Cape Cod, *The Marriage of Figaro*, set in an apartment in New York, and *Don Giovanni*, set in Spanish Harlem in New York, were televised by the Public Broadcasting Service (PBS).

Among his talents is providing motivation for his singers so they can produce more than just perfect notes. In a column in the *Los Angeles Times* on August 2, 2016, music critic Mark Swed wrote of watching Sellars work: "He didn't want much beautiful sound. He cared more about articulating the important words than the little ones. What mattered in every phrase was dramatic, namely human, motivation."

Sellars has taught at UCLA and directed productions around the world, including the premiere of John Adams's and Alice Goodman's opera *Nixon in China* and performances in major venues such as Lincoln Center in New York City. He has garnered numerous awards for directing theater and opera, and is known for helping vocalists reach their full potential.

At the first rehearsal, the director explains the basic requirements for the actors, which include showing up on time or slightly early for rehearsals and spending some time working on their parts when they are not at the theater. This work may be learning their lines or thinking about how best to express the feelings they are supposed to convey. The director then talks to the actors about his or her vision for the play and its setting and period. Next comes a complete read-through of the play.

The first read-through is just that—all the actors read their parts. No acting takes place at this point. The actors simply sit and read the play out loud from beginning to end. It is a good idea to have them sit

Prior to the first rehearsal, the director explains the vision for the play so actors can start thinking about how to best perform to achieve it.

around a table, as this makes it easier for them to make notes. As they read, the director may point out particularly important lines or moments in the play. This helps the actors understand what elements in the script they should emphasize.

The next type of rehearsal that the director undertakes is "blocking rehearsals." Since the set will not be completed for the early rehearsals, the director can either have temporary furniture in place, such as folding chairs for a sofa, and/or have the outlines of key pieces of furniture, doors, and the like, taped off in location on the stage. The blocking rehearsal is a run-through of the play with the director telling the actors where to stand, sit, move, and so on. The actors note the blocking in their script. The director is not usually autocratic about the placement of the actors. The actors themselves may have ideas about movements that enhance the performance. A good director welcomes ideas from the actors and considers them carefully. However, there may be some places in the play where the director wants to have the actors in a specific arrangement, called a "**tableau**," in order to make a point.

The director needs to understand the conventions of various types of plays. Different types of plays—comedies, dramas, and musicals—require specific skills from the director. Most of the plays a community theater produces will probably be comedies. Audiences are most likely to turn out for a comedy because they want to be entertained. In order to direct actors effectively, the director must understand how to deliver lines effectively by using pacing (the speed at which things happen), pausing, pitch, volume, and emphasis to elicit the most humor. A lot of comedy relies on running jokes, including certain repeated movements. Replication of movement—the same movement being repeated by several characters—is funny. Similarly, some comedies, both classic and modern, rely on characters going in and out of doors on opposite walls or using other pieces of the set. Thus, the director has to consider how best to incorporate the set into the blocking and understand the exact timing needed to make such jokes work.

Finally, the working rehearsals begin. The director undertakes what most people think of when they hear the word "rehearsal"—that is, the actors practicing particular scenes. During rehearsal, the director discusses various aspects of their performances with the actors. Every scene has a focus, and the director must discuss this point with the actors. He or she must lead the actors to understand and portray the relationships between the characters, what lines are key to getting the point of the scene across, what the characters are thinking, and how to use body language to express the characters' feelings. In a comedy, the director may have to work on the timing of the delivery of lines so that the jokes are properly set up. Every director has exercises he or she has learned over time to help actors deliver their lines for the best dramatic or comedic effect. Early working rehearsals typically concentrate on individual scenes rather than an entire act. Only after all the individual scenes are perfected does the director allow an entire act to be run through.

During rehearsals, the director focuses on one scene at a time, trying to perfect all its elements.

The director uses a variety of techniques to help the actors give the best performance possible. It is not the words that express the meaning of the play, it is the way the actors deliver them. Inexperienced actors are inclined to deliver their lines as if they were reading them out loud, with little feeling. Or they may read them in a set rhythm, especially if they are performing a piece set in a different historical period. For example, it is often difficult for the director to get young or inexperienced actors to deliver lines from one of Shakespeare's plays in a natural way. They tend to recite Shakespeare's lines like poetry, instead of emphasizing specific words the way they would in natural speech. Still another tendency is for actors to show that they are aware they are acting for an audience by declaiming their lines as if they were quoting them, instead of delivering them in the natural tone that they would use with people in real life.

It is the director's job to get the actor to understand the emotion the playwright's words are meant to convey and the motivations driving the character so the lines are delivered with meaning. In a comedy, a certain degree of exaggeration in presenting a character might add to the humor. In a drama, however, creating believable, realistic characters is important to getting the audience to identify with the characters, accept the premise of the play, and be carried along by the story.

The director is responsible for seeing that the actors speak and move in a way that enhances the believability of their characters. At times, this can be challenging. If one is directing a high school play and the characters are not high school students, the director is going to be faced with student actors who must convincingly portray people who are older than they are. It is possible to make a young person look like an adult through the use of makeup and costume, but the actor must also speak and move like a person of that age. The same applies to inexperienced actors playing characters from a different socioeconomic background. A successful businessman—or the teenaged son of the successful businessman—playing a sharecropper will need to adopt a way of speaking— and of moving—that is completely different from his usual way of talking and walking. It is the director's job to instruct the actors so that they realize these characteristics in the roles they are playing.

The director must imbue the actor with a sense of *why* the character is saying a line. Think of the word "OK," and how many different meanings it can have. One can say "OK" in a way that means "Enough! Stop pestering me!" One can say it with enthusiasm, meaning "Great!" One can say it with reluctance, agreeing to do something one doesn't really want to do. The director has to ensure that the actor understands the context for the lines and delivers them appropriately. This is especially true when working with inexperienced actors. One technique used by James Carver, an experienced community theater director, and described in his book *Carver's Manual on Community Theatre Directing*, is to have the actor visualize in his or her mind the situation the character is describing. The actor reads through a passage and sees it as if he or she were there. Then, when the character speaks, the actor delivers the lines with feeling.

When people are uncertain, they often find it easier not to look in the eyes of the person they are speaking to. It's often necessary for the director to reinforce the need for actors to look at each other and interact the way they would in real life. Directing also requires seeing that actors move in a way that is appropriate to the lines they are delivering. If two actors are having a fight, their bodies must be tense. It's not enough for an actor to clench her fist. It is the director's job to see that the actors use their whole bodies to reflect the tone of the confrontation. A **subservient** character might bow his or her shoulders and move in a **tentative** or **deferential** way, for example. The trick for the director is to get the actors to use their bodies naturally rather than move in an exaggerated fashion—except in certain **farces**, where such "hamming" is appropriate.

This brings up an important point. Different types of plays require different types of movement. A **slapstick** comedy, a romantic comedy, and a serious drama require different levels of realism in body movement. In some cases, amateur actors may have experience with certain types of plays, such as contemporary drama, and need pointers from the director on how to move for a **period piece** or broad comedy. As with comedy, plays set in historical periods can require the director to address the way the actors move. Today, most people, especially young people, wear comfortable clothing most of the time and move in a loose, free-flowing fashion. This was not true in earlier times, when clothing was often more formal and restricting. Looking natural in such clothing often requires one to maintain a better posture (or

Some types of plays, such as broad comedy and children's theater, require exaggerated, not realistic, movement.

frame). People of different classes moved differently. A workman in a Victorian setting might slump his shoulders and shuffle, whereas a gentleman would carry himself with good posture and move in a firm, deliberate manner.

Clothing often requires one to modify one's movement. A woman wearing a historical dress with stiff petticoats will have to learn to move naturally in her costume. For this reason, if actors are going to be wearing period costumes, or any other clothing with special characteristics, it's a good idea to allow them to try on and practice moving in such outfits. The players' actual costumes may not be finished until well into rehearsal, but it may be possible to give the actor a similar outfit to practice in, or to suggest practicing in clothing that will provide a similar feel.

The final stage of rehearsals is complete run-throughs of the acts of the play. By the time the director is ready to do complete run-throughs of the acts, he or she will demand that the actors be "off **book**." This means that the actors should have their lines memorized. (In reality, it's unusual for actors to remember their lines perfectly when they first go off book, so they often have to call for lines.) Being able to work without looking at a script means that they can look at other actors, elements of the set, and props as they will do during a performance. Now that they're not carrying scripts, they can use the props as they will during the performance. This allows the director to concentrate on how the characters relate to each other. The goal of run-throughs is to give the director a chance to observe the actors performing a complete act of the play. Typically, the director will let the actors perform the entire act, and then **critique** them, discussing issues that need to be addressed or changed. When correcting actors, a director needs to find something positive to say as well. That way, actors don't become discouraged, and they feel that the director is working with them rather than against them. A director has to be careful not to neglect those actors who are more experienced and doing a fine job. The inexperienced actors will need more attention, but it's natural for all people to question how well they are doing, and everyone needs positive reinforcement. Therefore, the director should always say something to all the actors, even if it's just "good job."

The final week before the show is devoted to full rehearsals. First, a full technical rehearsal takes place. At this rehearsal, all the technical elements—sets, lights, props, sound, music—are applied as they will be in the performance. The tech rehearsal takes place at the beginning of the final week so that any problems that are identified can be fixed in time for the performance. Prior to the technical rehearsal, the director goes over all the cues for changes of light, sound, set, and any other technical elements, with the stage manager, who will be in charge of overseeing the crew during the performance. The actors then perform the entire play as they will in the actual performance. During this rehearsal, however, the director does not concentrate on the actors, but on the crew. He or she makes sure that the crewmembers have all the cues down, and that the effects work properly. Actors also wear their costumes for the first time during the tech rehearsal. This gives the director the opportunity to see if there is enough time for costume changes, if alterations need to be made to the costumes, or if an actor needs more assistance to change a costume. All types of problems typically arise during the technical rehearsal, but that's what it is for. After the rehearsal, however, most of the problems that are likely to arise can be addressed.

The next few rehearsals are full rehearsals with the tech crew and actors, culminating in full dress rehearsals. Most directors call for two or three dress rehearsals on the days directly before the first performance. The dress rehearsal is a full performance of the play. Often the cast and crew are allowed to invite family or friends to the dress rehearsal. This gives the actors the opportunity to perform before an audience, and it gives the director the chance to see if the play is having the desired effect. After each dress rehearsal, the director gives notes to the cast.

The rehearsal process is more than work. It is an opportunity for the actors to be creative and enjoy themselves in a social activity. The people involved in school and community theater are volunteers. Therefore, the director must make the work pleasant, even while getting the actors to perform appropriately. Making the actors part of the creative process and encouraging them to express their opinions gives them a feeling of accomplishment and makes them more enthusiastic about the process.

Performance Night

On the night of the first performance, the director makes sure everything is ready and often gives the actors a pep talk, thanking them for all their hard work. Then it's show time. The director will watch the performance from the rear of the theater and take notes. If there are things the director wants to bring to the attention of the actors, he or she will tell the actors after the performance, or before the next evening's performance. It is the stage manager who typically runs the show during subsequent performances. In a small company, the director may continue to watch performances and give notes, either after each performance or at some performances.

Getting the Job Done

To be an effective director, one must constantly make decisions. Mastering decision making isn't easy, but the director needs to be **decisive**. There is a limited amount of time to rehearse and mount a play, so the director needs to be able to consider all the options and choose the best one. At the same time, the director needs to be flexible enough to adjust his or her preconceived ideas when the situation requires.

The director has to realize that he or she may not be able to achieve a perfect result. The actors will vary in their skill levels, and the creation of sets and costumes will be limited by budgetary constraints. A successful director will be able to get the job done well and the problems solved, even if the solutions aren't perfect. A successful director welcomes the contributions of the actors and crew, and is willing to incorporate their ideas when they seem likely to enhance the production. This openness to input ensures that the participants are willing to share ideas,

Actors perform a curtain call. Rehearsing the curtain call helps actors get the most positive response from the audience.

and it will give them a feeling that it is "their play," not just the director's. The feeling of satisfaction that cast and crew get from seeing their contributions used encourages them to work harder—and to participate in future productions. Finally, the director needs

to assess the progress of all elements of the play on a regular basis to ensure that everything is on schedule and developing along the lines he or she has envisioned.

The director may have to address issues such as providing access to the stage for mobility or vision-impaired performers.

CHAPTER FOUR

PITFALLS AND PROBLEMS

T here are many pitfalls and problems that can arise in the course of putting on a play. Issues can occur during the preproduction, production, or performance stages. Some of these pitfalls can be anticipated. Others will be completely unexpected.

Budget Issues

One of the biggest issues for community theater groups is not having enough money. Even if work is done by volunteers, materials must be purchased, lights and sound equipment rented, and halls paid for. It's important to make a budget before even beginning a play and to estimate how much everything is going to cost. Then add 10 to 20 percent to that amount. There is always something that was forgotten or that the director didn't know was needed until halfway through creating a costume, set, or other element.

If the group is a permanent organization with money in the bank from previous productions or other activities (such as giving acting classes to children), then the director knows how much money is available. Otherwise, unless the producer is willing to put up the money and recoup it from ticket sales, the funds have to be acquired. One way of doing this is to sell advertising in the program to local businesses. The businesses reap the benefit of publicity and the satisfaction of supporting local culture. Another way to raise funds is to solicit donations on a large or small scale. If the group is professional enough to have a board of directors, often these people are respected and affluent members of the community who have contacts with other affluent and respected people. The director should get the board members involved in fundraising. Use social media. Solicit donations on the group's Facebook page and website. Offer a discount to people who buy tickets to the show in advance. This will provide the group with working capital. Solicit funds through a crowdfunding site, such as Kickstarter. Offer a pair of tickets to anyone who donates a given amount of money, possibly combined with an invitation to an opening-night, after-show reception. Another approach, which can be combined with other fundraising methods, is to reduce the amount of money required by soliciting the lending or donation of materials and goods needed. It's unlikely one can get everything one needs this way, but everything obtained is something that doesn't need to be purchased. It is possible to apply for grants to fund community theaters, but in today's difficult economic environment, these are often hard to obtain unless a community theater is well established.

School productions have some advantages in the funding department, as they often have an auditorium with equipment they can use to put on a play. Parents of students may be willing to chip in and make costumes and donate material for sets. Students can raise additional funds by traditional techniques such as holding bake sales, yard sales, and car washes.

Audition Issues

Sometimes not enough people show up for auditions to fill all the roles in the play. There are a few ways to approach this problem, but the best solution is to hold further auditions. The worst solution is to recruit someone to play a role. An actor cast this way often has the attitude that he or she is doing the director a favor, which may lead to problems such as refusing to follow the director's instructions. Careful choice of a play can help avoid this situation. In school and community theater, plays with few characters and more women than men are preferable because more women than men generally show up for auditions. Also, when posting notices of auditions, include information about the gender and age of the roles. A retired older male actor may turn out for a community theater audition if he knows that there's an appropriate role for him. Get the word out as widely as possible that you are holding auditions. Send flyers or post them on bulletin boards at local college drama departments and other places with a lot of foot traffic, such as your local library.

If you are putting on a play in a public school, the student body probably includes youths of many cultural and ethnic backgrounds. If a play is cast with only white actors, this may be taken as a sign of prejudice and cultural insensitivity. Certain roles

Choosing a play that requires a culturally diverse cast enhances the experience for both student actors and the audience.

require a person of a particular ethnic background. For example, in the musical *South Pacific*, a young white lieutenant in World War II falls in love with a native girl on a Pacific island, which would horrify his family back home. This situation requires a white boy and an Asian girl. Another factor is that the white male, Lieutenant Cable, must be able to sing the beautiful but difficult "Younger Than Springtime." The choir director can inform the director if such a talent is a member of his chorus. However, many roles in plays can be played by people of any race, and sometimes by people of any gender. A sensitive director tries to encourage cultural diversity in his or her work.

Dealing with the disappointed is a problem often faced by directors. Those who don't get roles, or who get a supporting role instead of a leading role, may be disappointed and even resentful. The director needs to acknowledge their feelings. It's best to tell them honestly why they were chosen for the role they were given, rather than the one they wanted, and to stress that you are relying on them in their present role. If the group has a permanent pool of actors who put on plays, or a group of locals who put on most of them, try to rotate the lead roles. Obviously, this depends on the choice of play, but the director usually controls that choice or has significant input. If actors know from past experience that different people get the lead in different plays, they are more likely to accept not being chosen this time and will not feel that the director is playing favorites. In general, community theaters with a regular group of actors are less likely to be problematic in terms of roles because they tend to develop camaraderie. However, the director is like the parent in this theatrical family. He or she must make sure that all the actors receive acknowledgment for their contributions.

Problems with Actors

Inevitably there will be times when an actor doesn't work out. A person might continuously fail to show up for rehearsals. He or she might feel that performing in a play is not important because it is not a job. This behavior inconveniences the other actors and makes it impossible to put the play into shape. An actor might not be able to memorize his or her lines—or the actor may not feel he has to. The author once worked with a television actor. Based on his experience in television, he felt that it was not necessary to say the lines as they were written; for TV work, adlibbing something that approximated the meaning was good enough. Of course, this not only undermined the playwright's intent but made it difficult for the other actors to respond, since they rely on certain lines for their cues. Another problem that can arise is that some people simply cannot act, no matter how much direction they are given. The actor may still be struggling to emote and portray anything despite the director's best efforts to work with him or her. A person who shows up drunk or high cannot be kept in the cast under any circumstances. In these situations, the director may have to fire the actor.

The director needs to prepare in advance how to approach firing an actor, which needs to be done while there is still enough time to replace him or her. If it is necessary to fire an actor, it is best to take a nonconfrontational approach. Being confrontational not only creates bad feelings but can lead to an actor bad-mouthing the director and the play—and theater is a small world. You never know when you are going to run into the actor or someone who knows him or her. Instead, the actor should be told, "This is not working out. I know you're trying hard, but [*whatever the problem is*]." Often an actor who is struggling knows this and may even be relieved to be spared embarrassment.

A related problem is having an actor drop out of the show. It might be possible for the director to

FAULTY EQUIPMENT

No matter how often you test the equipment, there may come a time when it fails in performance. This can happen even in professional theaters. This happened to Shoshana Bean, the star of the musical *Wicked*. Bean was playing Elphaba, the character who will become the Wicked Witch in Oz. At the end of act 1, she is supposed to rise up on a **cherry picker** and "fly" while singing the signature song "Defying Gravity." The problem was that one night the cherry picker failed to operate. The actress left the cherry picker and sang the song on stage. However, the rest of the cast was supposed to end the big number by coming onstage and pointing up at her flying above the stage—which she wasn't. Their solution: run onstage and lie on the floor pointing up at her standing above them. Sometimes in theater you just have to improvise!

Shoshana Bean was grounded one night when a prop failed.

contact one of the other actors who auditioned and replace him or her. However, in some circumstances, especially if the actor is a man in his prime, there may not be any suitable replacement candidates. The director may have to resume auditions or contact actors he or she has worked with before.

Sometimes an actor—or a crewmember—will be surly or uncooperative. Often people become negative if they think that the work they are doing is not appreciated. Making a point of complimenting their work and giving them attention will often defuse this type of situation.

Onstage Problems

Problems will sometimes occur while actors are performing onstage. The most common problem is that an actor will forget a line. Teach actors how to deal with this situation during rehearsals when they are "off book." If an actor forgets a line, that is the time to discuss it. Often another actor in the scene can cover by responding to the unspoken line. (Actor One is supposed to say "I hate you," but can't remember that's her next line. Actor Two says, "I suppose you hate me," or "You look like you hate me." Often this is all it takes to get the first actor back on track.) Or, if an actor can't remember the exact wording, he or she can say something approximating the line. It is distracting to use a prompter during a performance, as it takes the audience's focus off the actors onstage.

If an actor is simply having trouble learning his or her lines, there are a variety of techniques that can be used to address the problem, such as having the actor visualize what he or she is describing or having the actor focus on one key word in the line. Most books on directing include "tricks" that directors can use to help actors learn their lines. To avoid having last-minute problems, check to make sure that actors with small parts have learned their lines well in advance of the full rehearsals. Those with small parts often think that they can wait until the last minute to learn their parts, only to find it takes more time to memorize them than they planned for.

A more serious problem can occur if an actor becomes ill or injured. The best approach in this case is to have another member of the company take the role, even though he or she will have to carry a script onstage. The fact that the actor has become sick or injured and that another actor will be taking his or her place should be announced. The audience will generally be supportive of this approach, and the person filling in will be familiar with the play and the intent of the scenes. Doing this is preferable to canceling the play and inconveniencing audience members. It's rare in community theater to use understudies because there are usually only a small number of performances. Understudies most likely will not have the chance to act, and the director will have the added work of rehearsing two people.

Making Sure an Audience Shows Up

After all the hard work everyone has put in, it's important to get an adequate audience for the play.

The payoff for all the actors' hard work comes when they perform before an audience.

Schools can rely on a core group of friends and parents to attend their performances. Well-established community theaters usually have a mailing list of people who have attended plays in the past. Often they plan their list of shows a year in advance and sell season tickets. A new or small group that puts on plays occasionally may have to work harder to get the word out about their play. For a community theater group or school play, the director is often involved in promoting the play. This usually involves writing a press release with information about the play and sending it to local newspapers. The director may

post information about the play on social networking sites, such as Facebook and Twitter, and/or the group's website. Making flyers is also useful. They can be posted in local businesses and distributed to residents in the neighborhood where the play is being performed. The director might want to do an interview with the local newspaper or radio station to publicize the show. To build a mailing list for future productions, the group may want to have a guest book at the entrance where people can write their name and address "to be informed of upcoming productions."

The director must make sure that there is a plan in place to safely evacuate the cast, crew, and audience in case of a natural or man-made disaster.

External Crises

Another problem that can occur in our violence-prone world is a national or international crisis or a natural disaster such as a hurricane or earthquake. If an event were to occur in the area where the play is being held, the play would be stopped and the company and the audience either told to shelter in place or evacuate. The proper approach would be to follow any instructions from the authorities.

What happens, however, when an event occurs in another location, but people should be informed about it? The author was interning at a major summer theater on the day that President Richard Nixon resigned from office. Unfortunately, at the time he did this, the theater was in the middle of a performance of a musical comedy. The director and producer were aware of what had happened, but the audience was not. They felt that this event, which could affect the United States in a major way, should be announced to the audience. However, they were uncertain, given the serious nature of the event and the frivolous nature of the play, whether it would be appropriate to continue with the performance. In the end, the director decided to announce what happened at intermission, and then continue with the show. The audience was, if anything, more responsive to the play during the second act, welcoming a respite from the disturbing news.

The skills learned in directing a play can be applied to directing a team in a business or professional setting.

CHAPTER FIVE

CAREER DIRECTION

You can gain many valuable skills from your experience directing school or community theater. The experience can also imbue you with confidence in yourself, knowing that you can lead a group of people and solve problems when they arise. The skills you learn from directing can be applied in two ways. First, you may decide that you want to pursue a professional career in the theater. Second, you may decide to pursue a profession unrelated to the theater that makes use of the skills you've acquired in the theater. In either case, the following are some of the ways you can apply what you have learned from your directing experience.

Pursuing a Theatrical Career

If you decide that you want to undertake a professional directing career, you will most likely want to pursue a degree in theater arts, directing, or a related area at the college level. Interning at a professional theater can provide you with a chance to work with a professional director and actors. You will probably not start out as a professional director but as an assistant to a director. You can use the knowledge you gained in community or high school theater directly in your new role, especially your skills in dealing with actors, and they will help you advance in the field. If you should get into directing professionally, it's a good idea to join the Stage Directors and Choreographers Society or Actors' Equity. Membership in these unions provides you with information about the field, contacts with professionals, and the right to work on union stages.

Real-World Careers

Most people who direct community theater groups do so part-time and maintain a day job in a business or profession. The nice thing about the skills you develop as a director is that they can be applied to any career in any field and will contribute to your success. Here are some of the ways they can be applied.

People Skills

In a real-world job, you will have to deal with superiors, coworkers, subordinates, and clients or customers. Working with actors, especially ones who are not being paid to put up with you, should have given you a knowledge of how to motivate people to do what needs to be done. The approach that will make you successful with subordinates and coworkers is the same one that makes you successful with cast and crew members: giving recognition and praise for their contributions when they do a job well, and criticizing them constructively, in a way

A manager explains his vision for a project in much the same that a director explains his or her vision for a play.

that is focused on fixing the problem, not chastising or embarrassing them in public. As in the theater, work is a collaborative effort, and soliciting ideas from coworkers and subordinates can make them feel like part of a team and also increase your pool of knowledge. If the people you work with feel that you respect them and value their contribution, then they are more likely to support you and do their best work for you.

In business, one has to deal with people in a range of jobs and from a range of educational, ethnic, racial, and socioeconomic backgrounds, an experience that is also true of the theater. In the role of director, a person has to learn to understand, communicate with, and get the best from different types of people. A director has to understand the motivations that drive characters in order to elicit authentic performances from actors. In the course of analyzing the characters in a play, the director learns much about people, and this knowledge contributes to the development of empathy and understanding. People can sense if a superior or coworker understands and cares about them, and they are more likely to respond positively to, work productively for, and cooperate with someone who they sense empathizes with them. In addition, having a sense of empathy gives one a better understanding of clients or customers. This understanding contributes to the ability to identify what they want or need, and it can assist a businessperson in making sales and establishing long-term relationships with clients.

Unfortunately, sometimes in the real world you will have to work with difficult people you can't fire, including superiors and customers or clients. There is nowhere like the theater to gain experience working with difficult personalities! By the time you get done directing a high school or community theater play, you should have the skills to calm a person who is upset about an issue and refocus the conversation on how to solve the problem. Given the fact that directing puts people in high-stress situations, going through the process should equip you to deal with stress in the business or professional arena without losing your cool.

Team-Building Skills

Leadership in the theater and in business is about making the group successful. The leader must often deal with people who have strong personalities and an even stronger desire to gain recognition and advancement. The leader must not only have an overall vision for a project but also motivate diverse people to embrace it. He or she must be able to imbue team members with the belief that to succeed they must all support and help each other, so that the project as a whole will succeed. Anyone who has worked as a director in the theater has been faced with the same problem. If each actor is out to stand out at the expense of the other actors, then the play will not come together and work as a whole. Therefore, the director must develop tools to get actors to work as a team for the good of the play, not just themselves. The techniques learned in the theater apply to the real world as well.

Communication Skills

By definition, the director in the theater works every day with words. One of the keys to success in business is the ability to communicate. One has to communicate effectively with subordinates and superiors. One has to make presentations to clients and customers as well as to senior management when trying to obtain

Making a successful presentation requires planning all the elements in advance and rehearsing it.

resources for a project. Such presentations need to be well planned and organized so that the key points are emphasized. Like a director, the manager must be able to analyze the audience and gear the presentation to that audience. The ability to use words and body language effectively can enhance one's chances of success. When constructing presentations, one has to be able to use images as well as words to influence the audience. The director's experience in creating a picture on the stage using visual elements as well as words can be applied to creating and delivering powerful presentations.

Project Management

Sooner or later you are going to be required to manage a project in the real world. Despite the fact that the venue is different, setting up and directing a project is very similar to directing a play. You must analyze the requirements for the project and establish what resources and people are required to accomplish it. Unless the project is being carried out solely by people who report to you, you will be faced with getting people in various departments to carry out the tasks required, including people who aren't under your authority. You will need to break the project down into discrete tasks and figure out when each task needs to be completed. You will then need to schedule people and resources and track them in order to ensure that everything is ready when it is required. This process mirrors very closely the process of directing a play.

Budgeting

Budgeting is a key aspect of business and professional activities. A play's director is required to make a budget and track expenditures to make sure that production costs don't exceed the amount

MAKING CHOICES

In an article in *Theatre Journal,* "10 Ways Being a Theater Major Prepared Me for Success," Tom Vander Well discusses the ways in which his theater experience prepared him for a career as a business consultant, and later a business owner. One of the skills that his theater background equipped him with was the ability to improvise. According to Vander Well, "Theater taught me how to focus, think quickly, and make do while giving the impression that you've got it all under control. It's served me well when clients, airlines, coworkers, or technology wreak unexpected havoc at the worst possible moment."

Another thing Vander Well learned was how to make hard choices. He talks of having to choose between an inexperienced jock who was right for the role and a schoolmate who was a personal friend who was less well suited but who might be offended if he didn't get the part. He also describes having to choose

of money that is available. Therefore, you will be familiar with how to do these tasks as well as when and how to address financial issues when they arise. Your experience as a director will also give you some skills in raising money. Even though you may be requesting funds from senior management rather than donors, you will likely have some experience in formulating a presentation on what you are trying to achieve with your project and justifying why you need funds for it.

whether to perform a play scheduled for an outdoor amphitheater outside in bad weather or to change the venue, which would mean having the actors perform in an unfamiliar environment for which they had not prepared their blocking. As Vander Well says, "Any business person will tell you that difficult decisions must sometimes be made. The higher the position the harder the decisions and the more people those decisions affect."

In short, in the theater one can not only learn but practice skills that will ultimately contribute to one's success. At the same time, someone can try different approaches and experience the results without risk because one's livelihood does not depend on the decisions made in this setting. This allows a person the freedom to make mistakes and learn from them, which contributes greatly to success.

Knowing how to create a budget doesn't ensure that one will have all the money one could wish. Most school and community plays are produced on a shoestring. The director must be creative to achieve the type of production he or she wants with limited funds. Many business and project managers find themselves in the same situation. The ability to get the results they want with a limited amount of money is a valuable skill that allows them to accomplish a lot with few resources.

Whether a lavish Broadway or local community theater production, every play requires advertising and marketing; such skills can be applied in business as well.

Time-Management Skills

Time management is a critical skill for getting things done. No one is under more time pressure than a director in the theater. Deadlines are inflexible. The show must go on at a set date and time. This forces the director to learn and use time-management skills. Working as a director means doing lots of multitasking. This means that the director must learn techniques for time management. Time management begins with making a to-do list with all the required tasks and ranking them in order of priority.

Two of the major faults common among managers are their refusal to delegate responsibilities and their insistence on micromanaging all aspects of a project.

A director learns to delegate responsibility for many aspects of a production to others and maintain a higher level of supervision, keeping track of their progress in general. This management style not only results in work getting done more efficiently, since more tasks can be done simultaneously, but also results in happier crew members because they feel trusted and empowered.

A director's experience teaches him or her that one always needs to include extra time to deal with the unexpected. Time management is more than making a schedule. Directors face a constant barrage of time-management challenges. They are constantly subject to interruptions and distractions as those working on various technical areas require their attention, as well as actors who need help with their parts. People who are late or who don't show up affect their plans, which must be dealt with. Directors must address the problems of people who are disorganized or unprepared, and still pull the entire project together for a successful performance. They are also faced with the need to balance these demands with those in multiple other areas. They have to balance the time they spend on producing the play with the time required for other school or work activities, and still have time to take care of themselves.

Public Relations, Advertising, and Marketing

In community theater, the director is often involved in the advertising and marketing efforts that promote the performance and attract customers. The director may be involved in creating advertisements for the play, writing press releases about the upcoming performance, and possibly giving an interview to the local paper. He or she may have gained experience doing physical or electronic mailings. If a person works in an area such as marketing, he or she may be involved in special events for customers or the general public. The process of producing a special event is very similar to the process of producing a play. It involves planning all the aspects of the event, hiring all the vendors and equipment required, and overseeing the production of the event.

Overcoming Obstacles

Directing a production means doing whatever needs to be done with whatever resources are available. Rarely in school or community theater does the director have every resource he or she would like. The director must work with the people who are available to act and to do the technical work. He or she must work with the materials that are available to make sets and scenery. This approach requires the director to be flexible and adaptable.

The director must be able to see what could be done with the resources available and with the characteristics and talents of the people who are available to play roles in the play. It is the director's job to make the best that can be made of the actors he or she works with. This ability to use the resources at hand to the best effect possible is invaluable in business. In business, one can't always choose who is working on a project, but one can analyze what their strengths are and how to employ them to the best advantage.

Finally, being a director gives one experience in working hard for long hours. The end result is **ephemeral**. After weeks or months of hard work, the play will run for a limited number of performances. The actors will then **disperse**, the props will be put away, the rented equipment returned, and the sets torn down. In business, one is often called on to work long hours under tight deadlines to produce a report or presentation. Experience in working hard to achieve a goal helps one achieve goals in a timely fashion. And after the fact, when the emphasis moves on to the next project, this will be a familiar experience.

Being a director is a creative and fulfilling avocation. In addition, it is an excellent way to learn a range of skills that can be used to enhance one's performance in a business or profession.

Directing a community or school play develops skills that will serve you well in the future.

GLOSSARY

audition A tryout for a role in a performance.

avant-garde Unorthodox or experimental.

avocation A hobby or minor occupation that someone pursues after work and family responsibilities are fulfilled.

blocking The placement and movement of actors on a stage.

book The script of a play.

business The activities an actor engages in while onstage in a role.

callback A request for an actor who has auditioned for a role to come back for another reading.

cherry picker A machine with a bucket that holds and lifts people.

critique To analyze a play or performance.

decisive Making decisions resolutely and without hesitation or change of heart.

deferential Showing respect to someone else, especially by an underling to a person of authority.

disperse To distribute or spread over a wide area.

ephemeral Fleeting, impermanent, lasting a very short time.

farce A type of broad comedy marked by buffoonery, ridiculous situations, and characterizations that are crude.

harmoniously Working well together, free of discord.

ingenuity The skill to solve problems or be inventive.

motivate To give people a reason to perform an activity.

period piece A play set in a specific time period.

preconceive To make up one's mind in advance.

preproduction The preparation period before a director begins rehearsals.

reinforce To strengthen or support, sometimes through encouragement.

set The stage scenery and props such as furniture.

slapstick A type of comedy that relies on physical humor.

subservient Showing excessive deference to another person.

tableau An arrangement of actors on the stage.

tentative Hesitant, unsure, lacking confidence; the opposite of decisive.

usher A person who shows audience members to their seats in a theater.

FOR MORE INFORMATION

Books

Campbell, Drew. *Technical Theater for Nontechnical People.* 2nd ed. New York: Allworth Press, 2004.

Carver, James: *Carver's Manual on Community Theatre Directing: A Step-by-Step Approach.* Kalamazoo, MI: Hansa-Hewlett Publishing, 2010.

Chandler, Wilma Marcus. *Directing Theater 101: 10 Steps to Successful Productions for New Directors and Regional Theater Companies.* Hanover, NH: Smith and Kraus, 2008.

Jordan Moore, Susan. *"More Fog, Please": 31 Years Directing Community and High School Musicals.* Seattle, WA: CreateSpace, 2015.

Kaluta, John. *The Perfect Stage Crew: The Complete Technical Guide for High School, College, and Community Theater.* 2nd ed. New York, Allworth Press, 2016.

Mills, Daniel B. *Coaching Pre-Broadway Actors: Stress Free Strategies for Directors Who Have a Day Job.* Seattle, WA: CreateSpace, 2015.

Online Articles

Caird, John. "Want to Be a Theatre Director? Here Are My Top 10 Survival Tips." *Guardian,* March 23, 2010. https://www.theguardian.com/stage/theatreblog/2010/mar/23/theatre-director-10-top-tips.

Snetiker, Marc. "10 Big Broadway Disasters According to Seth Rudetsky." *Entertainment,* November 4, 2014. http://www.ew.com/article/2014/11/04/10-big-broadway-disasters-according-to-seth-rudetsky.

Vander Well, Tom. "Wayfarer's Journal: 10 Ways Being a Theatre Major Prepared Me for Success." *Theatre Journal,* January 12, 2012. https://tomvanderwell.wordpress.com/2012/01/16/10-ways-being-a-theatre-major-prepared-me-for-success.

Videos

Directors 2011
https://www.youtube.com/watch?v=xZg-EdoMtc0
Four directors talk about subjects such as getting started in the business; choosing their projects; and how they approach auditions.

How to Be a Director
https://www.youtube.com/watch?v=yBu255CjJyk
This video discusses how a director can adapt to actors' ways of working to get the best from them.

Websites

American Association of Community Theatre
http://www.aact.org
This organization serves those involved in community theater; its website features resources, job postings, and networking information.

The Art Career Project: Getting Started as a Theater Director
http://www.theartcareerproject.com/become-theater-director
The Art Career Project offers information on becoming a theater director, including expert advice and educational information.

Theaterfolk: Directing the High School Play
Part One: https://www.theatrefolk.com/spotlights/directing-the-high-school-play-part-one
Part Two: https://www.theatrefolk.com/spotlights/directing-the-high-school-play-part-two-the-rehearsal-process
These issues of the e-publication cover a wide range of topics and exercises for directors of high school plays.

INDEX

ABOUT THE AUTHOR

Jeri Freedman has a BA from Harvard University. She is the past director of the Boston Playwrights' Lab, an organization that produced original plays in Boston, Massachusetts. Her play *Uncle Duncan's Delusion* was published by Baker's Plays (now part of Samuel French), and her play *Choices*, cowritten with Samuel Bernstein, was staged at the American Theatre of Actors in New York City. She is also the author of more than fifty young adult nonfiction books.